Contents

The Champ!

Each week in NASCAR, one driver wins the race. But NASCAR has two kinds of champions. Each year, one driver comes out of the pack as the season-long NASCAR champion. The champions profiled in this book combined driving talent, **endurance**, and a little luck to become not just champions, but legends.

The Old Days

NASCAR was founded in 1948 by a group of drivers in the South. NASCAR stands for National Association for Stock Car Auto Racing. The drivers wanted to organize what had been an unorganized series of races. They created a system in which drivers earned points for how they finished in each race. Those points were added up and at the end of the season, and the driver with the most points was declared the Grand National champion. The first champion was Red Byron, who won a pair of races in 1948 to capture the season title.

Other champs in those early years included Herb Thomas (1951 and 1953), Tim Flock (1952 and 1955), and Buck Baker (1956 and 1957). Flock set a NASCAR record with 18 race wins in 1955, a record that stood until 1967 when Richard Petty blew it away with 27 wins.

Today's Champions

From 1972 until 2004, the NASCAR champion won the Winston Cup, named for a major **sponsor**. The points system gave drivers bonuses for race wins, laps led, and races finished.

Among NASCAR's early heroes were two-time champ Herb Thomas, "Fireball" Roberts, and Curtis Turner.

Great NASCAR Champions

JIM FRANCIS

2002
WINSTON CUP CHAMPION
STEWART

JOE GIBBS RACING

x1000r/min

CRABTREE PUBLISHING COMPANY
www.crabtreebooks.com

Crabtree Publishing Company

www.crabtreebooks.com

Coordinating editor
Chester Fisher

Series and project editor
Shoreline Publishing Group LLC

Author
Jim Francis

Project Manager
Kavita Lad (Q2AMEDIA)

Art direction
Rahul Dhiman (Q2AMEDIA)

Design
Ranjan Singh (Q2AMEDIA)

Cover Design
Ravijot Singh (Q2AMEDIA)

Photo research
Anasuya Acharya & Amit Tigga (Q2AMEDIA)

Manuscript development and photo research
assistance provided by Shoreline Publishing
Group LLC, Santa Barbara, California

Acknowledgments

The publishers would like to thanks the following for
permission to reproduce photographs:

Associated Press: pages 4, 6; Robert Baker: page 24;
    BH: page 10 (bottom); Dave Martin: page 21;
    Chris O'Meara: page 11; Bill Scott: page 13
Bettmann/Corbis: page 8
Nascar Media: page 27; Nick Laham: pages 28-29;
    Todd Warshaw: page 25
Neil Rabınowitz/Corbis: page 20 (bottom)
Joe Robbins: pages 9, 10 (top), 12, 14-19, 20 (middle right),
    22-23, 26, 30-31
Robbins Photography: Nigel Kinrade: page 5;
    Brian Spurlock: cover, title page
State Library and Archives of Florida: page 7

Cover: Tony Stewart won the NASCAR Winston cup
Championship, 2002. Joe Gibbs racing.

Title page: Tony Stewart won the NASCAR Winston cup
Championship, 2002. Joe Gibbs racing.

Library and Archives Canada Cataloguing in Publication

Francis, Jim, 1963-
    Great NASCAR champions / Jim Francis.

(NASCAR)
Includes index.
ISBN 978-0-7787-3187-0 (bound).--ISBN 978-0-7787-3195-5 (pbk.)

    1. Automobile racing drivers--United States--Biography--Juvenile
literature. 2. Stock car drivers--United States--Biography--Juvenile
literature. 3. NASCAR (Association)--Juvenile literature. I. Title.
II. Series: NASCAR (St. Catharines, Ont.)

GV1032.A1F73 2008   j796.72'092273   C2007-907374-3

Library of Congress Cataloging-in-Publication Data

Francis, Jim, 1963-
  Great NASCAR champions / Jim Francis.
      p. cm. -- (NASCAR)
  Includes index.
  ISBN-13: 978-0-7787-3187-0 (rlb)
  ISBN-10: 0-7787-3187-1 (rlb)
  ISBN-13: 978-0-7787-3195-5 (pb)
  ISBN-10: 0-7787-3195-2 (pb)
  1. Stock car drivers--United States--Biography--Juvenile literature. 2. Stock
car racing--United States--Juvenile literature. 3. NASCAR (Association)--
Juvenile literature. I. Title.
  GV1032.A1F67 2008
  796.72092'2--dc22
  [B]
                                        2007049019

Crabtree Publishing Company

www.crabtreebooks.com   1-800-387-7650

Published in Canada
Crabtree Publishing
616 Welland Ave.
St. Catharines, ON
L2M 5V6

Published in the United States
Crabtree Publishing
PMB16A
350 Fifth Ave., Suite 3308
New York, NY 10118

Published in the United Kingdom
Crabtree Publishing
White Cross Mills
High Town, Lancaster
LA1 4XS

Published in Australia
Crabtree Publishing
386 Mt. Alexander Rd.
Ascot Vale (Melbourne)
VIC 3032

In some cases, the championship was not decided until the final race. However, in many cases, the champion clinched his title with many races left to go. To prevent that from happening, and to increase fan interest in races at the end of the season, NASCAR changed the way it decides its champs. Beginning in 2004, the "Chase for the Cup" started. Now, drivers earn points throughout the season, as before. However, before the final 10 races of the season, the top 12 drivers in points are put in a separate "Chase" group. Only a driver in that top 12 has a chance at the season title. Their points are recalculated so that the drivers are bunched close together. Then, the driver with the most total points after the 10 races is the champion. (The trophy was renamed the Nextel Cup from 2004-2007 and the Sprint Cup beginning in 2008, both thanks to a major sponsor.)

NASCAR Then and Now

Lots of things have changed from NASCAR's early days to today. Perhaps the biggest changes came in the cars. In the early days, the drivers often drove regular cars that they also used in their everyday lives. Today, drivers and race teams only use high-tech cars created especially for the racetrack. Another big difference is that races are held all over the United States instead of just on Southern tracks.

Jimmie Johnson won the 2006 and 2007 Nextel Cups by roaring through the Chase!

The King of NASCAR

NASCAR has created many legends over the years, from its moonshine roots to today's champions. But one driver set the stage for all of the legends to follow: Richard "The King" Petty.

Richard Petty: The King

In most sports, there is one athlete who stands head and shoulders above his competition. In NASCAR, that athlete is Richard Petty. Known simply as "The King," Petty owns more all-time records than any other driver—most championships (tied with 7) most wins (200) most starts (1,184), and many more. Petty's success on the track for more than 30 years played a huge role in turning the sport from a small Southern series into an international success story. Before Petty came along, most NASCAR fans lived in the South, and few national newspapers or television stations covered the sport. Petty's outstanding driving skills and winning personality took the sport into the future. He remains the longtime symbol of the sport—hard-driving, tough, yet humble. His story mirrors those of many drivers, but his record is something that they all still try to match.

Petty's 1968 Plymounth didn't yet have the famous blue-and-red paint scheme of later years.

 6

Like Father, Like Son

Richard Petty started out working with his father, Lee. The elder Petty was one of the top drivers in NASCAR's early years. Cars and engines were a big part of everyday life in the Petty household. Richard's brother, Maurice, became a top engine expert and crew chief. Richard went to dozens of races with his dad, helping in the pits and learning how to race. By attending so many races, the younger Petty got a view of racing that few others of his generation enjoyed. His understanding of racing techniques, his knowledge of engines and tires, and his understanding of different tracks all combined to help him throughout his career. Richard kept practicing—and working—and he was itching to get behind the wheel for a real race.

Lee, however, made Richard wait until he was 21. He wanted to make sure that Richard learned the business of racing, and all the behind-the-scenes jobs first. Finally, in 1959, Richard started in his first NASCAR race. It was the beginning of one of sport's most impressive careers. Richard was named the 1959 NASCAR rookie of the year for his many high finishes and great racing skill. One of the highlights of that season for the young driver was driving against his father in many races. He also got to watch Lee win the first Daytona 500 in Florida, a race that would become the most important on the NASCAR calendar. In that first season, Richard chose the number 43 for his car, following the number 42 car driven by his dad. In 1960, Richard won the first of his record 200 career race victories, in a 100 mile (160.9 km) event in North Carolina.

Here's a young Richard Petty in 1964 accepting his trophy for winning the Mountaineer 500 race. Miss West Virginia handed him the trophy.

Lee Petty

Though Lee Petty didn't start racing until his mid-30s, he made up for lost time quickly. Lee was the first driver to win three NASCAR titles (1954, 1958, and 1959). In 1959, he also won the first Daytona 500. Lee retired in 1964 with 54 race victories, which was the most at the time. In 1967, another driver passed that mark—a driver named Richard Petty, Lee's hard-charging son. Lee also got to watch his grandson, Kyle, and great-grandson, Adam, race in NASCAR.

A Fast Start

That first win got Petty rolling . . . by 1962, he was regularly among the leaders in the annual championship race. That year, he won nine races and just barely missed winning his first title, finishing second behind veteran Joe Weatherly. The younger Petty was gaining notice for his high-speed style and ability to succeed on all types of tracks. In 1963, Petty finished second again, even though he won 14 races. The next year, he really broke out. He started the season by winning his first Daytona 500. He roared around the world-famous track in a new record average of more than 154 miles (247.8 km) per hour.

He and Lee thus became the first father-son team to win that important race. They added another milestone at the end of the year, as Richard matched his dad as a NASCAR champion. It was the first of seven NASCAR titles in his career, a number that would later be matched only by the great Dale Earnhardt Sr., and approached only by Jeff Gordon, who has four titles.

Smash and crash! Petty (43) flies by on the high side during this NASCAR crash. Avoiding trouble is a great way to win.

Beginning in 1972, Petty's No. 43 car took on this famous blue-and-red paint design, based on his new sponsor, the STP oil company.

"THE RACER'S EDGE"

A Fight with NASCAR

In 1965, Richard and his race team got into a fight with NASCAR over their car. Though he was the champ, he was still looking for anything that would make him faster. Into his powder blue No. 43 car, he put a newly designed type of engine, known as a "hemi." The powerful engine was not used by other NASCAR racers, and the organizers said that it gave Petty an unfair advantage. They ruled that he could not use the "hemi" in races. In protest, the champ took a seat, but not behind the wheel. Petty sat out races in the first half of the season. Finally, NASCAR changed its mind, and Petty returned for the second half of 1965. He kicked off the 1966 season with another Daytona 500 win (he would end up with an all-time record seven Daytona 500 wins), but lost the season title to longtime **rival** David Pearson. Though he was not yet 30, Petty was already one of NASCAR's legends, with two season titles and dozens of race wins. But not even he would have predicted what happened next (see box).

One Amazing Year

In 1967, Richard Petty put together one of the greatest single seasons in any American sport. He took part in 48 races . . . and won 27 of them! He finished in the top five in all but 10 of the 48 races. Beginning in mid-August, he won a record 10 races in a row! Petty became NASCAR's all-time leader in races won, too, overtaking his dad's total of 54. His third season championship was by the largest margin in history, not surprisingly. It was such a dominant performance that he earned his famous nickname: The King.

Petty Owns the '70s

Petty won the 1971 season title and then helped change the sport again. In 1972, he joined with STP, a company that made engine-care products. Sponsors had been around for years, but Petty made them an even bigger part of the sport. With STP as its major sponsor, his team had new resources to stay on top of the sport. Petty's car was painted red, white, and blue to match the STP colors, and his success helped make No. 43 nationally famous. The entire sport was sponsored by a cigarette company, and the champion now earned the Winston Cup. All this new attention brought TV into the sport. More and more races were shown to larger and larger audiences. Throughout the 1970s, NASCAR got more and more popular. Meanwhile, Petty just kept winning: He won a total of five championships in the 1970s (see chart), a feat matched by no other driver in a single decade. He even finished second in two other years. As the 1980s began, Petty was still winning—including such important races

as his seventh Daytona 500 in 1981—but not as often. Younger drivers in faster cars were catching up to The King. In 1984, he won his final race, No. 200 in his career, at the Firecracker 400 held at the Daytona International Speedway in July, with President Ronald Reagan in the stands.

Wearing his famous feathered cowboy hat, Petty watches his race team compete.

Another crown for The King: Here's Petty crossing the finish line to win the 1971 Daytona 500.

A Farewell Tour

Petty announced that 1992 would be his last as a driver. At each stop on the Winston Cup season that year, he enjoyed special celebrations. The Richard Petty Fan Appreciation Tour was as much to thank his fans as for his fans to cheer him one more time. Petty was voted the Most Popular Driver nine times by NASCAR fans. His broad smile and winning attitude made him a hero to millions. In his last race, he crashed his car, but he shrugged it off . . . "That's racing," he said.

Petty's Championship Seasons

Year	Race Wins
1964	9
1967	27
1971	21
1972	8
1974	10
1975	13
1979	5

The King Today

Petty continues to be a big part of NASCAR today, mostly as the owner of the Petty Enterprises racing team. In 2007, the team ran the cars of Bobby Labonte and Richard's son, Kyle. They also had cars in NASCAR's second **circuit**, known as the Busch Series. Away from the track, Petty is still a hero, but for a different reason. He and Kyle have raised millions of dollars to help create several summer camps for children facing serious illnesses. The kids come for a summer of fun and to forget, for a while, that they're sick. Though Petty hasn't been behind the wheel of a racecar for over 15 years, he remains The King of NASCAR. There may never be another driver like him.

At every stop on his farewell tour, Petty was thanked by the fans who had followed his every move on the track.

The Silver Fox

Sometimes, it takes a great personality to make a great champion; other times it just takes a guy who likes to win. David Pearson was not the flashiest guy on the track, but he sure could race. The South Carolina native provided the perfect rival for NASCAR's 1960s hero, Richard Petty.

A Rival for Petty

If not for Richard Petty, David Pearson would be NASCAR's top winning driver. The man they called "The Silver Fox" won 105 races in his 27-year career behind the wheel, second only to Petty. Throughout the 1960s and 1970s, the two ace drivers often battled neck-and-neck for the checkered flag. In fact, they finished 1-2 in an amazing 63 races . . . and Pearson won three more of those than Petty did.

Southern Star

While Petty hailed from North Carolina and racing royalty, Pearson was from South Carolina and a humble background. He started out on small dirt tracks and made it to NASCAR's top level in 1960, when he was rookie of the year (as Petty had been the year before). He improved steadily. In 1966, he won his first of three NASCAR season championships, winning 15 races and finishing in the top 10 in 33 of 48 races. Petty's 1967 success overshadows the fact that Pearson won the titles in 1968 and 1969. His 16 race wins in the 1968 season were the second-most by any driver in the years after Petty's famous 27 wins in 1967. Of course, Petty has the other high totals—18 in 1970 and 21 in 1971.

Pearson's second-best-ever total of 105 race wins included this one in 1976 at Charlotte, North Carolina.

A Regular Winner

While Petty holds the record for most total victories, Pearson is top at winning percentage. That is, more wins per start than any other driver, taking the checkered flag more than 18 percent of the time.

Two Great Moments

Every rivalry like this one has moments that make it special. For Pearson and Petty, there were two. The first came in the 1974 Firecracker 400. On the last lap, Pearson seemed to suddenly slow down as if having engine trouble. Petty raced ahead, but the Fox pulled a trap. Slipping quickly behind Petty, Pearson used a move called a "**draft**" to slingshot around Petty just before the finish line and win the race. The second was in the 1976 Daytona 500 and ended with Pearson's only win in that great event. Again, he and Petty were dueling on the last lap. Just at the final turn, they collided, spun out, and the cars ended up on the infield in smoke. While Petty couldn't restart his car, Pearson managed to roll his battered vehicle across the finish line. It was one of racing's classic finishes. Pearson retired in 1986, but remains a NASCAR legend, linked forever with his rival Richard Petty.

Cale Yarborough's 83 race victories are fifth-most of all-time.

Three Straight

Only one driver has ever won three NASCAR titles in a row: Cale Yarborough. In between Petty's 1975 and 1979 titles, Yarborough pulled off his "threepeat" (1976, 1977, and 1978). The South Carolina native also finished second three times and won four Daytona 500s.

The Man in Black

Few athletes in any sport enjoyed as much fan support as our next champion, Dale Earnhardt Sr. The winner of seven NASCAR titles, matching Petty's record total, Earnhardt was the face of NASCAR for the 1980s and 1990s.

The Family Business

Dale Earnhardt started his road to the top like Richard Petty did: in the family garage. Ralph Earnhardt, Dale's dad, was a top driver in the 1950s. Ralph won more than 500 races of all kinds, from short-track races on dirt to convertible races on Florida's hard-packed beaches. Ralph inspired Dale to drive and to drive hard. "I was always at his side," Dale Sr. remembered. "I wanted to see what made his cars and his driving so strong."

Earnhardt started driving himself as a teenager on small tracks in his native North Carolina, but he always had his sights set on NASCAR. He drove in local stock car races, while also working in garages after school. He also started a family at a young age; his son Kerry was born when Dale was only 17. Sadly, Ralph passed away in 1973, before Dale really got his start driving stock cars.

When Earnhardt got a new sponsor in 1986, he got a new nickname. The Goodwrench company's paint colors—and Earnhardt's rough personality—led to "The Man in Black."

Young Man in a Hurry

Earnhardt drove in his first NASCAR race in 1975. He finished 22nd, just ahead of another young driver named Richard Childress, who would soon play a huge role in his life. Earnhardt raced at the top level only a few more times before finally landing a full-time job in 1979. For car owner Rod Osterlund, he won his first race in 1979 at the Southeastern 500 in Tennessee. Earnhardt was also named the circuit's rookie of the year. A gruff young man with a thick mustache, Earnhardt was almost a perfect example of a quiet and determined young Southern racer. Fans expected big things of him. In 1980, only his second full season, Earnhardt delivered. He won five races and earned his first of seven NASCAR titles (tied with Richard Petty for most ever). He got the first of his two famous nicknames at about this time for his take-no-prisoners style. The driver they called "Ironhead" made a big move in 1984, switching for good to the new Richard Childress Racing (RCR) team, headed by his former fellow driver. Together, the duo would make history.

Though Earnhardt would make his No. 3 car world famous, he began his racing career in the No. 2 car owned by Rod Osterlund.

Dale Roars Ahead

With Childress, Earnhardt moved into the famous No. 3 car that he would turn into a legend. After two top-10 finishes, Earnhardt broke through in 1986 with his second NASCAR championship. In 1987, he repeated the feat, becoming the third driver with three titles. Almost as important, RCR got a new sponsor in Goodwrench. The No. 3 car was painted black to match the company's colors, and Earnhardt got his second and most famous nickname: The Man in Black. Earnhardt added a black helmet and dark racing goggles. Add in his typical grimace and his signature mustache, and you had the ultimate picture of the rough-and-tumble racer.

Bump and Run

Earnhardt earned another nickname thanks to his famous racing style. In NASCAR, it's not illegal to bump into another car in an effort to get past. Drivers can be inches from another car at very high speeds around the track. It's just a part of the style of stock car racing. Earnhardt, however, played this game at its highest level. It was a rare race that didn't end with his car dented and banged up. He was able to nudge, bump, and push his opponents with his high-speed battering ram. From this powerful style, he was called "The **Intimidator**."

Richard Childress joins the Earnhardt family— Dale, Dale Jr., and Teresa—in 1987.

Out of the way! Earnhardt (No. 3) was never afraid to use his bumper to move cars out of his way.

This way of driving was not really illegal—though sometimes Dale did bend the rules to win a race. It made some fellow drivers mad, but it thrilled fans who loved the "paint-rubbing" slam-bang action.

What a Record!

The period from 1986 to 1994 was a remarkable one for Earnhardt. He finished in the top three in seven of those nine years, while winning six of his seven career NASCAR titles. In 1993, he clinched the title in the final race of the season. His last championship came in 1994, tying him with the great Richard Petty. It was perhaps the greatest single decade in NASCAR history and made him a hero to "NASCAR Nation."

Dale Jr.

In 1999, the Earnhardt family racing legacy continued. After winning the 1998 Busch Series title, Dale Earnhardt Jr. joined NASCAR's top level, racing side-by-side with his famous dad. Dale Jr. won his first race in 2000 and earned three top-10 season finishes through 2007. He struggled to live up to his father's reputation, but his humble style helped make him a fan favorite. After Dale Sr.'s death in 2001, Teresa Earnhardt took over the family race team. But in 2008, Dale Jr. left that team and joined up with his father's old car owner, rival Hendrick Motorsports.

Finally...Daytona

While Earnhardt had earned nearly every honor that NASCAR could offer, a win in the mighty Daytona 500 **eluded** him. He ran the race 20 times before he could finally enter Victory Lane. His emotional win in 1998 remains one of NASCAR's signature moments. On his victory lap, crews from all 43 teams lined pit road to shake his hand. Dale capped off his late-career surge with a second-place overall finish in 2000. He had reached $41 million in career earnings, an all-time best at the time. His 76 total wins were among the most ever. His fans filled every track with their black No. 3 t-shirts. And his son Dale Jr. was continuing to rise in the ranks of NASCAR. Everything was going Earnhardt's way.

A Tragic End

Then, suddenly, it was all over. In the 2001 Daytona 500, the first race of the season, Earnhardt was in third place, watching as his teammate Michael Waltrip headed toward victory. But on the final lap, an accident sent Earnhardt's car spinning. Another car hit Earnhardt, and he crashed into the wall nearly nose first. He was killed instantly. Racing and sports fans mourned the loss of their hero. His death led to many safety improvements in NASCAR racing. Dale Jr. returned to the track that summer to win another race at Daytona in memory of his dad.

Son ahead of father: For the last three years of his life, Dale Sr. (black car) got to race against Dale Jr. (red car) and the two became closer.

18

Earnhardt's Championship Seasons

Year	Race Wins
1980	5
1986	5
1987	11
1990	9
1991	4
1993	6
1994	4

The Legend Continues

Dale Sr.'s seven titles and his amazing popularity continue to make him one of NASCAR's most popular figures. Though he has been gone for nearly seven years, sales of his souvenirs continue to be very strong, and you can't go to a race without seeing fans wearing No. 3 shirts and hats. Of course, Dale Jr. continues to carry the famous name to the track each week. His name also remains on the Dale Earnhardt Inc. (DEI) racing team that he started late in his life. Dale Jr. raced for the team, as did Waltrip and other drivers. Dale Sr.'s power in the sport led him to want to be an owner as well as a driver. After his death, however, Dale Jr. and stepmother Teresa didn't get along, and Dale Jr. left the DEI team in 2008. Dale Sr.'s legacy is set, however. There will never be another Man in Black.

Finally! Dale Sr. celebrates with his crew after winning the 1998 Daytona 500.

The Rainbow Warrior

In 1994, the year that Dale Earnhardt Sr. won his seventh title, the next great NASCAR champion was just starting out. That year, Jeff Gordon began one of NASCAR's greatest careers.

On the Road

Jeff Gordon was born in California, a long way from the center of NASCAR Nation. He got his start racing small go-karts at local fairgrounds. He would end up with more than 600 victories in races on small tracks throughout his youth. A trip to Indiana when he was nine changed his life. He saw the Indy cars racing at the famed Indianapolis Motor Speedway. Indy cars are **open-wheel** cars, a somewhat different style of car and racing than NASCAR. After the family moved to Indiana, Gordon rose quickly. By the time he was a teenager, he was racing sprint cars, which are smaller racecars, on tight, dirt tracks. When he was 19, he became the youngest national champion in the history of quarter-midgets, which are one step below the Indy level. A ride in the Indy 500 looked like it was in Gordon's future.

A young Jeff Gordon first gained a love of racing watching open-wheel cars like these, shown at the 1989 Indy 500.

A Move to NASCAR

When Gordon was 19, he went to a driving school in North Carolina and drove a stock car for the first time. "Once I drove it, I knew it," he said. "I knew that was what I wanted to drive." It was a good decision. In his first year in stock cars, Gordon won 11 races at NASCAR's Busch Series level and was the rookie of the year. By 1993, he was a full-time racer at the top level and was named the rookie of the year. He won his first race at that level in 1994 and finished eighth overall. (Gordon put together an amazing streak: from 1994-2004, he never finished out of the top 10 in season points.) He also won the first NASCAR race held at the Indianapolis Motor Speedway, the place that had inspired him as a youngster. Jeff Gordon was a young man in a hurry.

Young, good-looking, and a great driver, Gordon had a hard time making fans like him as much as their older, tougher favorites.

21

Suddenly, a Champ

Going into the 1995 season, Gordon was expected to challenge for the championship. NASCAR fans used to the "good ol' boy" attitude of drivers like Dale Earnhardt Sr. were slow to warm up to the driver they called "Wonder Boy." Many fans didn't like that the young driver was beating their old favorites. But beat them he did, and in 1995, he won his first NASCAR championship. At 24, he was the youngest driver in the modern period of NASCAR (since 1972) to earn that honor. He won seven races that year and finished in the top ten 23 times, while earning more than $4 million. The Wonder Boy had made it to the top.

The Kid and the Veteran

Meanwhile, the rivalry between Gordon and older drivers was heating up. In 1995, in fact, Earnhardt finished only 34 points behind Gordon, thus losing out on a chance to top Richard Petty's seven championships. Earnhardt famously said that Gordon would "have to drink milk" to celebrate his title, instead of the traditional champagne. In 1999, they had their toughest tussle on the track. It came at the Daytona 500. Gordon was in the lead, but for the final 10 laps, Earnhardt was breathing down his neck. The **veteran** tried all his tricks to make a pass, but the kid held him off for another big win. "That was the longest ten laps of my life!" Gordon said afterward.

Jeff posed with his wife Brooke after he won the 1997 NASCAR Winston Cup trophy.

Two More Titles

In 1997, Gordon added another "youngest ever" title. At only 26, he won the famed Daytona 500 for the first time. The wins just kept on coming for Gordon. In 1997, he won 10 races and his second NASCAR title. He repeated the feat in 1998, winning a career-best 13 races. That was tied (with Richard Petty) for the best total since 1972. As a three-time champ, Gordon had earned his place among the sport's great drivers, regardless of what all of Dale Earnhardt's fans thought.

Gordon's pit crew in action: Can you count the nine pit crew members who can go "over the wall" to help get Gordon gassed up and ready to go?

Rainbow Warrior's Pit crew

Gordon got a lot of attention because of his car, too. He was sponsored by the Glidden Paint Co., and they chose a multi-colored design for their car. Thanks to that, and the cool uniforms worn by his **pit crew**, Gordon's team became known as the Rainbow Warriors. Working with owner Rick Hendrick, Gordon and his team were dominant on the track and in the pits.

Gordon Keeps Racing Ahead

Gordon won his fourth championship in the 2001 season, though he won only three races. His steady driving continued to be the key to his success. He was aggressive when he needed to be, but he worked very hard to stay near the top, rather than take chances. He was also part of the very successful Hendrick team that included former NASCAR champ Terry Labonte. The veteran Labonte was a big help to Gordon as the young driver was getting started. But by 2001, Gordon had grown into a **mentor** to younger drivers like Jimmie Johnson.

Trouble off the Track

The years after his fourth title were somewhat difficult for Gordon. The anti-Gordon forces seemed to be growing, especially after Dale Sr. was tragically killed in a wreck at the beginning of the 2001 season. When Gordon won the title the same year, many fans rejected him as a hero. In 2004, NASCAR changed the way in which its champions were determined. Had NASCAR gone by the old system, Gordon's record that year probably would have earned him another title. As it was, he finished third overall. Off the track, his marriage to his wife Brooke was breaking up, and they would divorce in 2003. With Gordon in the public eye, this private difficulty was especially hard. In 2004, he led the way entering the "Chase for the Cup," but couldn't hold on to the lead and wound up finishing third. In 2005, he had perhaps his worst season, finishing 11th and losing his longtime crew chief, Robbie Loomis. An 11th place finish would have been good for some, but not for Gordon.

After several difficult years, Gordon rebounded in 2007. Here, he poses with his new wife Ingrid—one of the reasons that things were looking up for him. Gordon won six races in 2007 and continued his quest to match the awesome championship totals of Petty and Earnhardt.

Gordon Today

Though he has not won a season title since 2001, Gordon continues to be one of NASCAR's top drivers. Plus, in 2006, he married model Ingrid Vandenbosch, and they had daughter Ella in 2007. Meanwhile, he continued his many charitable activities, mostly through the Jeff Gordon Foundation. On the track in '07, he overtook his old rival Dale Earnhardt Sr. when he won his 77th career race (Gordon finished 2007 with 81 career wins). He also led the points race most of the season. In the season-ending 10-race "Chase for the Cup," Gordon slipped to second place behind teammate Jimmie Johnson. However, still a "young" driver who is not yet 40, Gordon has a good shot at adding to his record as one of NASCAR's greatest all-time drivers.

Here's one of NASCAR's most familiar sights—Jeff Gordon's rainbow car roaring to take over first place in a race.

Gordon's Championships

Year	Race Wins
1995	7
1997	10
1998	13
2001	6

25

Today's Champions

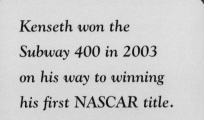

Since the beginning of the 2000s, NASCAR has had only one repeat champion. More and more drivers are challenging for the championship—and the Chase for the Cup continues! Let's meet some of today's former (and future) champs.

Matt Kenseth

Wisconsin is known more for its cheese than producing NASCAR drivers, but that's just where 2003 champion Matt Kenseth grew up. Kenseth had a love of motors and cars from an early age. As a teenager, he restored a sports car just in time for his 16th birthday, and Kenseth was soon winning races in his own car. Kenseth won many events across the Midwest in various sorts of small cars. His big break into the big time came in 1997. An old pal from the Midwest circuits, Robbie Reiser, needed a driver for a NASCAR Busch Series car that he was organizing—and he wanted Kenseth. Kenseth got off to a fast start, nearly winning the Busch Series in both 1998 and 1999, while also getting some rides on NASCAR's top level. He made the jump to full-time in 2000 and was the rookie of the year (beating out a young driver named Dale Earnhardt Jr. for that honor!). In 2002, Kenseth had the most wins in the series, and in 2003, he went all the way to the top. Though he won only one race, he was a regular among the top five, ending up there in 25 of 36 races. That gave him enough points to earn his first NASCAR championship. Not bad for a "cheesehead." Kenseth was also a part of the first four "Chase for the Cup" competitions.

Kenseth won the Subway 400 in 2003 on his way to winning his first NASCAR title.

Kurt Busch

Kurt Busch has a name that sounds like a racer. His family name is the same as NASCAR's second series, but there's no relation. Busch started racing in small stock cars called "featherlites" in his native Nevada. He was the Southwest region champion when he was only 19 in that series. He moved up to driver on the NASCAR Craftsman Truck series before moving to NASCAR's top level in 2001. That's right, Busch skipped (for the most part) Busch! Driving for veteran owner Jack Roush, Busch got his first win in 2002 on his way to a third-place overall finish. He got there with a late rush, winning three of the last five races of the year. Two years later, he won it all. In the first year of the "Chase for the Cup," he had nine top-10 finishes in the 10 Chase races and roared to the season title. Though Busch has gotten in trouble for some mistakes while driving, he's certain to be among the stars to watch in the years ahead.

Several sets of brothers have raced in NASCAR, but only one can say that they each won a title. Terry Labonte (left) won in 1984 and 1996, while younger brother Bobby (right) was the champ in 2000.

Family Champs

NASCAR has a long family history—families of drivers, that is. Here's a list of some of the more famous NASCAR families. An * by a name means that driver won at least one NASCAR championship.

Fathers and Sons

Bobby*, Davey, and Clifford Allison

Buck* and Buddy Baker

Dale* and Dale Earnhardt

Ned* and Dale* Jarrett

Lee and Richard* Petty

Richard* and Kyle Petty

Brothers

Bobby and Donnie Allison

Geoff, Bret, and Todd Bodine

Jeff and Ward Burton

Terry* and Bobby* Labonte

Darrell* and Michael Waltrip

Rusty*, Mike, and Kenny Wallace

Tony Stewart

If it's got wheels, Tony Stewart has probably raced in it . . . and won! Stewart has won two NASCAR championships (2002 and 2005) but winning national titles is nothing new for him. The driver they call "Tony the Tiger" has been a winner since he could reach the gas pedal.

Long Road to the Top

Tony grew up in Indiana. He raced first in low, small vehicles called "karts." By the time he was 12, he was a national champ in his age group. He moved up to a series of sports cars. In 1995, he became the first driver to win national titles in three different sports car divisions in the same year. To accomplish this feat, Tony had to race both days on nearly every weekend in tracks all across the country. But he was a young man on a mission and his "Triple Crown" win that year made many top-level car owners sit up and take notice. However, Tony didn't make the move to NASCAR. Instead, he went into open-wheel racing in the Indy Racing League. He was the rookie of the year in that series, and seemed all lined up for a great career in open-wheel racing. But like Jeff Gordon did before him, Tony made the switch to stock cars. NASCAR's Joe Gibbs Racing hired him to join NASCAR in 1998.

That year, Tony won 22 races in the Busch Series and joined NASCAR's top series (then called the Winston Cup) in 1999. That began an amazing run of seven straight finishes in the top 10 in points. Tony's wide experience in racing helped him succeed at all of NASCAR's tracks. In 2002, he topped all his other accomplishments when he won his first NASCAR title. He did it again in 2005, earning an amazing $13 million! Stewart missed the Chase for the Cup the next year, but put together a very solid 2007 season, winning three races and earning a spot in the Chase. Though he couldn't recapture his championship form, his hard-charging style and great team will make a force for years to come.

Tony Stewart drove this familiar orange-and-black No. 20 car to a pair of NASCAR championships as the only repeat winner in the 2000s.

Where does the money come from?

NASCAR drivers all want to take home the huge trophies that come with winning races. (And there are some weird ones, including giant cowboy boots, an electric guitar, and a gold-plated brick!). But they also compete for huge cash prizes. The actual winnings go to the race team's owner. Race teams can each run up to four cars in NASCAR's top level, and they use the winnings to help pay for the cars and the crews. Drivers usually get a very high salary, based on their successes in the past. So when you see Jeff Gordon hold up a giant check for winning a race, don't think that he gets all of that money to spend on baby toys for his new daughter. All of this money comes from two main areas: sponsors who put on the races to help promote their products, and television, which pays NASCAR for the rights to put the races on TV.

Jimmie Johnson

Few drivers have been as successful in the 2000s as Jimmie Johnson has. The Californian did not finish below fifth in the season-long points race from 2002-2007. He capped off that run with NASCAR championships in 2006 and 2007.

From the Desert to the Track

Johnson started racing early, jumping on **motocross** motorcycles when he was just four. He became a top driver in several off-road racing series in the early 1990s. Off-road racers bounce over courses that wind through the desert, often dodging cacti and coyotes along the way! Some off-road races are run in football stadiums. Event organizers pile tons of dirt onto the fields to create mounds, humps, and jumps for the drivers to bounce over. Johnson proved to be a star in both the stadium and in the desert. He won six national titles in different off-road racing series, including the Mickey Thompson

Stadium Truck Series and the SCORE Desert championships. Johnson was also racing sports cars, and his success there caught the eye of NASCAR. After success in the Busch Series, in 2001, he joined Rick Hendrick's team. There he got great advice from his new teammate, racing legend Jeff Gordon.

Always Near the Top

By 2002, he was a regular winner on the top level of NASCAR. In both 2003 and 2004 he finished second overall. He showed his ability to race in all conditions, with top finishes in races on superspeedways, intermediate (medium-length) tracks, short tracks, and road courses. In 2002, he helped win the Race of Champions, in which he teamed with Gordon and a British motorcycle champ. They competed in each of their specialties, and the best combined time won.

He's No. 1: Jimmie Johnson, in the No. 48 car, was the 2006 NASCAR champion and made it two in a row by winning it all in 2007.

He Does It Again!

In 2006, after five straight top-five finishes in the season points list, Johnson finally broke through. He finished the Chase for the Cup with a win and four second-place finishes in the final 10 races. That let him vault from fifth to first by the time that the season was over. Look for Johnson among the leaders every year. In fact, he continued his success in 2007. With five victories before the Chase for the Cup began, he got even hotter once the Chase started. Johnson won five of the 10 Chase races, including four in a row. With a win in Phoenix, he took over the points lead and held on during the final race in Miami. Johnson became the first repeat champion since his Hendrick Motorsports teammate Jeff Gordon won two in a row in 1997 and 1998.

From 2004 through 2007, champions on NASCAR's top level received this trophy, the Nextel Cup. Beginning in 2008, the name will change to the Sprint Cup, because the main sponsor company's name changed.

Champs = Winners

A new NASCAR champ will be crowned every November after the final race of the Chase for the Cup. He'll get his big award at a banquet held each December in New York City. (It's a treat for big-city race fans to see their favorite NASCAR stock cars rolling through taxi-filled Times Square to pose for pictures!). The drivers who stand up there to get their big trophy, whether they have won one championship or many, whether they came from racing royalty or points west, all know that any driver can win a race. But they also know that it takes dedication, patience, and skill to win a NASCAR championship.

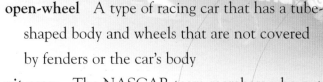

Glossary

circuit A series of competitions held in different places

draft A racing move in which one car follows very closely behind another, with the car in front cutting down the wind resistance for the car behind

eluded Escaped from

endurance The ability to stick with something for a long time

intimidator A person who, by their actions, causes others to feel scared or worried

mentor A wise and trusted teacher or counselor

moonshine A type of liquor

motocross A type of race run on off-road tracks

open-wheel A type of racing car that has a tube-shaped body and wheels that are not covered by fenders or the car's body

pit crew The NASCAR team members who put on new tires, fill a car with gas, or do other tasks when the driver pulls in for service

quest A long journey with a specific goal at the end

rival Competitor

rookie A first-year competitor in a professional sport

sponsor A company that pays an athlete to promote its product

veteran A person who has a lot of experience or practice in an activity

Index